Cutting-Edge Medicine

Connie Goldsmith

LERNER PUBLICATIONS COMPANY
MINNEAPOLIS

Lerner Publications Company
A division of Lerner Publishing Group, Inc.
241 First Avenue North
Minneapolis, Minnesota 55401 U.S.A.

Website address: www.lernerbooks.com

Library of Congress Cataloging-in-Publication Data

Goldsmith, Connie, 1945–
    Cutting-edge medicine / by Connie Goldsmith.
        p.   cm. — (Cool science)
    Includes bibliographical references and index.
    ISBN-13: 978–0–8225–6770–7 (lib. bdg. : alk. paper)
    1. Medicine—History—Juvenile literature. 2. Medical innovations—History—Juvenile literature.
    I. Title.
    R133.5.G65 2008
    610—dc22   2007001946

Manufactured in the United States of America
1 2 3 4 5 6 – JR – 13 12 11 10 09 08

3940

Table of Contents

Introduction

id you ever see the 1966 movie *Fantastic Voyage?* Scientists shrink a team of doctors and put them into a man's body. The doctors race in a tiny submarine through the man's bloodstream to his brain. There they zap a deadly blood clot.

Sound like science fiction? It is. But scientists are turning what was once impossible into reality. Some medical wonders are already in use. We can transplant arms and faces (move them from one body to another). We make useful drugs from lizard and bat spit. We can keep someone alive with fake blood.

Other medical wonders are on the way. In the next few years, we may cure many diseases by fixing sick genes. (Genes are tiny chemical instruction codes inside our cells. Cells are the tiny building blocks that make up our bodies.) We may also use genetic information to prevent many health problems.

It hasn't happened yet, but someday humans may be able to stay underwater like dolphins.

People could grow new organs using their own stem cells. And you might stay underwater like a dolphin with the help of tiny oxygen balls in your blood!

Health care will change more in the next ten years than it did in the last fifty years. Read on to see how cutting-edge medicine may give you a longer, healthier life.

chapter 1

Amazing Medicines

Since ancient times, healers have given sick people some weird stuff. Egyptians washed feverish bodies in urine. The Chinese used silkworm waste to cure some illnesses. If you had a headache in England one thousand years ago, you might slurp a tasty mixture of berry juice, cow brains, and goat waste.

We've come a long way since then. Modern doctors help sick people in ways ancient healers never dreamed of. Some medicines are still pretty weird. Drugs made from mold can cure strep

This recipe from 1550 B.C. comes from an ancient Egyptian medical document called the Ebers Papyrus. The recipe combines herbs with magic spells.

IT'S A FACT!

In 1928 a scientist named Alexander Fleming noticed that a bit of mold had killed bacteria (a kind of germ) growing in one of his lab dishes. The mold was the source of the first antibiotic (drug that fights bacteria), penicillin.

Alexander Fleming (*above right*) noticed that this mold killed bacteria in one of his lab dishes (*above left*).

throat. Drugs made from chicken pox germs protect against those very same germs. Scientists keep looking for medicines that help people live longer and healthier lives. And they're finding them in some strange places!

Open Wide

Animal spit, anyone? It may be gross, but it makes great medicine.

The Komodo dragon is the world's biggest lizard. About sixty different dangerous bacteria live inside its mouth. The animal's gums cover its sharp teeth. So when a Komodo dragon bites into a juicy goat, it slices through its own gums. But the lizards don't get sick from these germy cuts when they eat. They don't get sick when they bite one another either.

This Komodo dragon shows off its sticky spit as it waits for lunch— a white rat.

Scientists wondered why. They went to the Komodo's home in Indonesia and got samples of its gooey spit. They studied it and found that the spit kills many bacteria that make people really sick. Some of these bacteria are so strong that none of the drugs we have can kill them. A drug company is working to make a new antibiotic from Komodo dragon spit.

More than eighteen million Americans have diabetes. When people have diabetes, their bodies aren't good at turning sugar into energy. Too much sugar builds up in their blood. The extra sugar hurts the brain, heart, and kidneys. Because so many people have di-

IT'S A FACT!
Gila monsters can eat one-third of their body weight in one meal. That's like a fourth grader eating a burger the size of a beagle! Gila monsters eat only a few times a year. They live off fat stored in their tails the rest of the time.

abetes, a new diabetes drug is very valuable. It's big news. And when the new drug is made from Gila monster spit, it really gets noticed!

The Gila monster is a poisonous lizard. It lives in the desert in the southwestern United States. Scientists found a chemical in the lizard's spit that slows down food digestion. A drug made with this chemical helps diabetic people control their blood sugar. Some diabetics weigh too much. This drug also helps them lose weight. Who knew a grumpy lizard could be so useful?

The Gila monster is named for Arizona's Gila River basin. This is one place where the lizard lives.

Another amazing new medicine is made from vampire bat spit. Vampire bats bite other animals to drink their blood. The bat's spit has a chemical in it that keeps blood from clotting (forming a clump to stop bleeding). This lets the bat take as long as it needs to drink its meal.

People who have strokes can use this clot-busting spit too. A stroke is when a tiny blood clot gets stuck in a blood vessel in the brain. Blood carries oxygen all over the body. A blood clot in the brain can kill part of the brain by blocking its oxygen supply. Clot-busting drugs break up clots so blood can flow freely. Most clot-busting drugs work only within three hours of a stroke. The bat spit drug works up to nine hours after a stroke. It can help more people survive strokes with less brain damage.

Vampire bats drink blood from animals. Their spit has a chemical that keeps blood from clotting, which can help stroke victims.

Creepy Crawlies

What if you woke up after surgery and saw a couple of fat leeches on your arm?

Until the last century, doctors used bloodsucking leeches and flesh-eating maggots to treat their patients. They stopped nearly one hundred years ago, when better treatments came along.

Maggots and leeches are making a comeback. Maggots eat up rotting skin around a germy wound. This helps it heal faster. Leeches suck out extra blood around tiny stitches, like on a reattached finger. This keeps blood clots from forming. It gives the body time to get blood flowing normally to the finger.

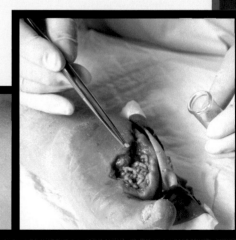

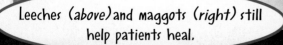

Leeches (*above*) and maggots (*right*) still help patients heal.

Groovy Vaccines

When a germ attacks you, your body makes proteins called antibodies to fight the germ. You might get sick, but the antibodies help you get better. They stay in your body after that. When the same germ attacks you again, the antibodies fight it off. This time you don't get sick.

Doctors use harmless parts of germs to make drugs called vaccines. When you get a vaccination, your body thinks a dangerous germ is attacking. You make antibodies to fight the germ. But you don't get sick, because the vaccine isn't a real germ. The antibodies keep you from getting sick if the real germ ever does attack you.

Before scientists invented vaccines, common germs often killed people. Vaccines have saved millions of lives. They prevent diseases such as polio, measles, and smallpox. In fact, the smallpox vaccine worked so well, it wiped out smallpox around the world. Kids no longer get the smallpox vaccine.

IT'S A FACT!

In 1796 Edward Jenner rubbed pus from a cowpox blister into cuts on the arm of eight-year-old James Phipps. (Cowpox is a disease similar to smallpox but less dangerous.) Six weeks later, Jenner proved that exposing the boy to cowpox protected him from deadly smallpox.

Some viruses (a kind of germ) can cause some kinds of cancer. Vaccines that help your body fight those viruses also protect you from cancer. One virus causes a disease called hepatitis B. Getting hepatitis B can lead to liver cancer. Another virus, called HPV, doesn't usually make people sick. But it can lead to cervical cancer (cancer of the womb opening) in women.

Babies have been getting the hepatitis B vaccine since 1982. Girls nine years and older can get an HPV vaccine. These vaccines help prevent kids from getting liver and cervical cancer when they grow up.

Scientists are also testing a vaccine to help prevent a kind of leukemia (blood cancer). Someday vaccines may prevent many kinds of cancer. It would be a lot easier to prevent cancer with vaccines than to treat cancer after people get it.

About forty-six million adults in the United States smoke cigarettes. Cigarettes contain a chemical called

IT'S A FACT!
Doctors say someday vaccines will be given with skin patches. Instead of giving you a shot, a nurse or doctor will plop a big sticky bandage on your arm.

Children can get vaccines that protect them from getting certain nicotine. Smokers feel good when the nicotine reaches their brains. It's hard to stop doing something that feels good. Smokers get addicted to nicotine. (An addiction is a habit that's hard to break.) Each day four thousand kids try smoking. Many of these kids end up addicted to nicotine.

Smoking causes heart and lung disease. Most smokers want to quit. But their addiction makes it hard to stop. Scientists are testing a vaccine for nicotine addiction. The vaccine helps people make antibodies against nicotine. The antibodies keep nicotine from reaching the brain. This means smoking doesn't feel good anymore. If testing goes well, the vaccine could help millions of people stop smoking.

The disease AIDS is caused by a virus called HIV. At least thirty-nine million people around the world have AIDS. About one million Americans have AIDS. Forty thousand more Americans get it each year. Scientists are working hard to make an HIV vaccine. HIV vaccines have worked on animals. In 2005 doctors began testing human vaccines. They think it may take ten years to make a safe vaccine for people. Someday kids may get HIV shots along with their other vaccines.

IT'S A FACT!

Scientists are trying to grow foods that contain vaccines. Think how much easier it'll be to eat a banana than get a shot!

chapter 2

Surprising Transplants

octors have tried for a long time to save lives by replacing weak kidneys, hearts, and livers. They've used organs from dead people and live people. They've used organs from animals. They've even made fake organs. Doctors can transplant more than twenty body parts, such as hearts, livers, and skin.

Transplants are tricky. It's hard to perfectly match someone who needs a new body part with someone who can give it (a donor). Most people who get transplants

In 2001 Maria Alvarez (center) received a partial liver from her son, Jose Alvarez, and a kidney from her daughter, Rosario Proscia. It was the first transplant involving two organs and three people.

must take strong drugs the rest of their lives. If they don't, their bodies might reject (attack) the new parts.

Even though transplants are tricky, a lot of people need them. There are more people who need new body parts than there are donors. Thousands of Americans are waiting for kidneys. Thousands more need new livers. Many of these people will die while they're waiting. Scientists are looking for better ways to give people the transplants they need.

IT'S A FACT!

Your liver does many important jobs for you. It clears poisons from your blood. It makes chemicals that help your blood clot. The liver is an unusual organ. It can regrow a cut-off part. This means living people can give parts of their livers to other people.

Small but Mighty

A lot of kids are waiting for heart transplants. It's hard to find hearts for very young children because their chests are so small. Doctors are trying some amazing things to save these tiny patients. Meet Camila and Serafina, two toddlers who got help at a California hospital.

Two-year-old Camila's heart problem made her weak and small for her age. She was so sick that doctors thought a heart transplant would kill her. Instead of giving her a transplant, they sewed a second heart from a baby into Camila's little chest.

The hearts pump separately. Each is growing bigger as Camila grows up. Transplanted hearts last ten to twenty years. Camila may need another transplant before she starts high school. At that time, doctors will trade her two hearts for one.

Two-year old Serafina's heart was so weak that doctors said she'd live just a few weeks. Her name went on the heart transplant waiting list. But her heart stopped working while she was waiting.

Doctors opened Serafina's chest. They attached a small pump to her heart. The pump kept her alive for eight weeks. Doctors found a tiny new heart for her. A few days after her transplant, Serafina sat up in bed and played with her parents.

From Sadness to Hope

In November 2005, a twelve-year-old Palestinian boy named Ahmad was shot in the head. Ahmad died. His father chose to give Ahmad's organs to other people.

Ahmad's heart went to a twelve-year-old girl. She'd been waiting five years. His lungs went to a fourteen-year-old girl with lung disease. One kidney went to a five-year-old boy, and the other went to a four-year-old girl. Ahmad's liver was divided. One half went to a baby and the other to a woman.

One donor like Ahmad can help several people. People who want to give their organs to others after they die carry organ donor cards with them. This way, health care workers will know their wishes.

Animals Helping People

Because so many people need transplants, scientists have turned to animals for help. Doctors have put hearts, livers, and kidneys from chimps and baboons into people. But the animal parts were too small to keep people alive. In 1984 a newborn known as Baby Faye got a baboon

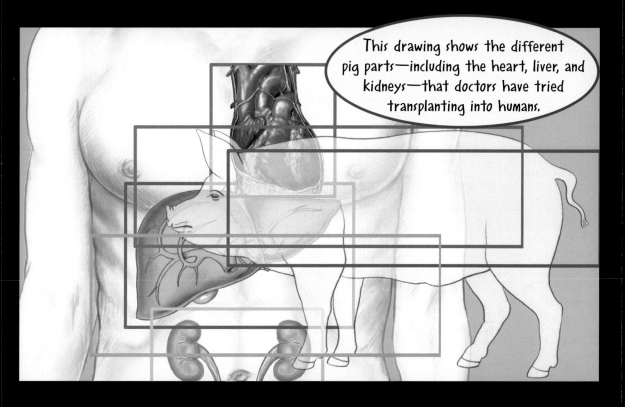

This drawing shows the different pig parts—including the heart, liver, and kidneys—that doctors have tried transplanting into humans.

heart. She lived twenty days with it. Then her body rejected it, and she died. Doctors haven't tried that on anyone else.

Human bodies are less likely to reject pig parts than body parts from other animals. Doctors put about sixty thousand parts from pig hearts into human hearts each year. They've also used cells from baby pig brains to treat Parkinson's disease. This is a brain disease that makes people stiff and shaky. Scientists have put human genes into a small group of pigs. They hope they can use more parts from these pigs in human bodies. People waiting for new livers have used livers from these pigs for a short time.

Next scientists may try putting human genes into other animals. Some-day people might grow their own spare parts inside animals. Imagine a barnyard filled with pigs and sheep. Each animal wears a tag: *John*

Smith's new heart or *Jane Doe's new lungs.* When it's time for Smith's transplant, he and the pig growing his heart go to operating rooms. Doctors take out Smith's bad heart. They replace it with the pig's heart. (This means that the pig dies.) Because the heart contains Smith's own genes, his body doesn't reject it.

Fake Blood

Blood carries oxygen from the lungs to every part of the body. People can die if their bodies don't get enough oxygen. This can happen if someone bleeds too much during an accident or operation. Each year, about eight million people donate blood to people who need it to stay alive.

Even so, often there's not enough blood to go around. Why? First: Blood lasts only forty days in special refrigerators. Second: There are eight different types of human blood. People can die if they get the wrong type. It's tricky to keep the right blood types on hand at all times.

This man is one of many people worldwide who donate blood every year.

To solve this problem, scientists have made fake blood. It lasts one year or more. It doesn't have to stay cold. It works in people with all blood types. It's perfect for places such as ambulances and battlefields, where workers can't keep real blood on hand.

IT'S A FACT!

In 1667 a French doctor did the first known blood transfusion. He put sheep's blood into a human. The poor person died!

Several big U.S. hospitals are trying out fake blood on people. Some ambulance workers are giving people fake blood to keep them alive until they reach the hospital.

Face-Off

Imagine wearing a dead person's face! Some people with badly hurt faces will soon be able to get face transplants.

French doctors did the world's first face transplant in 2005. They moved a dead donor's nose, lips, and chin to a woman named Isabelle. Her nose and lips had been bitten off in a dog attack. The transplant worked very well.

Doctors in the United States and Europe plan to try full face transplants. In this operation, doctors peel the face off a dead person. They also take the muscles,

This photo shows Isabelle Dinoire of France in November 2006, one year after she became the world's first person to receive a partial face transplant.

blood vessels, and nerves. Then they peel off the patient's damaged face and carefully attach the new face.

Like other people with transplants, people who have face transplants must take drugs for the rest of their lives. The drugs keep their bodies from rejecting their new faces.

What does a transplanted face look like? It depends a lot on the bones under it. Some doctors have practiced face transplants on dead people. They say a transplanted face looks more like the person who gets it than the person who gives it. But it's not exactly like either person.

chapter 3

Tinkering with Genes

Genes are why a bird has feathers and a bear has fur. Genes make one cat striped and another spotted. Genes are why you don't look like your friends and why you do look like your blood relatives. Genes give you straight black hair or curly red hair, brown eyes or blue. They make you tall, short, or in-between.

Genes are tiny chemical bundles inside all cells. Genes tell the cells exactly how to do everything your body needs to live. You get your genes from your mother and father. If you're adopted, your genes are from your birth mother and father.

Genes are the reason that blood relatives, like this family, have similar features.

But genes don't always work right. They may carry diseases from parent to child. Even healthy genes can mutate (suddenly change for no reason). Scientists believe gene mutations cause cancer.

Every day scientists learn more and more about genes. As they learn, they keep coming up with new ideas for using genes to help people live longer, healthier lives.

Gene Therapy

Scientists know that sick genes cause many health problems. Some of the most common are cystic fibrosis and muscular dystrophy. Sick genes also cause sickle-cell anemia, Down syndrome, and Tay-Sachs disease.

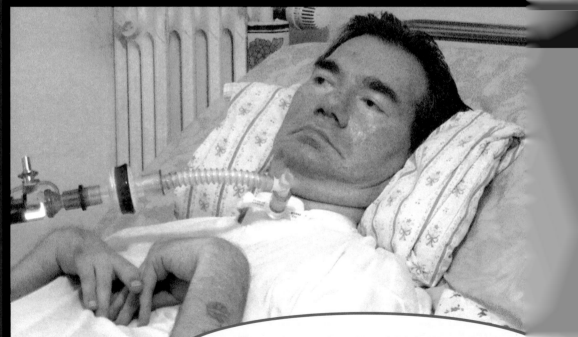

This man has muscular dystrophy, a genetic disorder that weakens skeletal muscles.

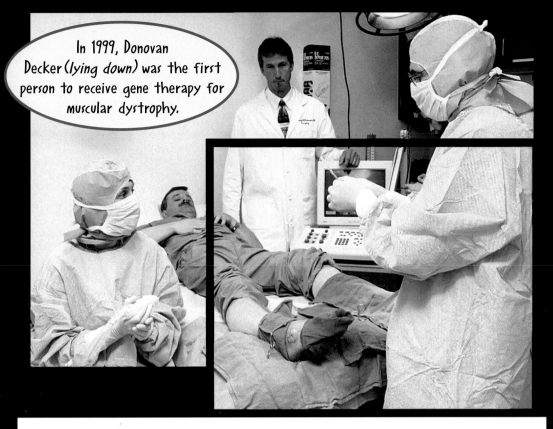

In 1999, Donovan Decker (*lying down*) was the first person to receive gene therapy for muscular dystrophy.

Think of a sick gene as a wrong word in the middle of a page. One wrong word can ruin a story. One sick gene can make someone sick. If we fix the wrong word, the story makes sense. And if we could fix the sick gene, children born with it could grow up healthy.

Gene therapy treats diseases by swapping sick genes with healthy ones. Doctors can use gene therapy to tell a body how to fight some kinds of cancer. They're also trying gene therapy to treat AIDS.

Gene therapy is very complex. It's so new that doctors use it with only a few patients at special hospitals. Gene therapy can have deadly side effects. Doctors use it only in people they can't help in other ways.

To replace sick genes, healthy genes must first get into the body. Scientists use viruses to carry genes into cells. They often use the virus that causes the common cold. They remove the parts of the virus that make people sneeze and cough. This leaves a hollow shell. Then scientists put healthy genes inside the shell. Doctors put the virus-and-gene package right into the body part that needs it.

Even though the virus shell can't give someone a cold, it can still make someone sick. The body often sees it and the genes inside it as invaders. When that happens, the body fights the virus and the strange genes so hard, it makes itself sick. This is called an immune reaction. It happened to eighteen-year-old Jesse Gelsinger in 1999. He died four days after getting gene therapy for liver disease.

Scientists are looking for ways to prevent immune reactions in gene therapy patients. They're trying other kinds of viruses and ways of masking viruses. They're even trying new ways to deliver genes that don't use viruses at all.

Since 1999 French doctors have treated several "bubble babies" with gene therapy. Bubble babies are children whose

David Vetter, shown here at age five in 1976, was known as "the boy in the plastic bubble." David had severe combined immune deficiency, which means his body couldn't fight germs.

bodies can't fight germs. Doctors replaced their sick genes with healthy ones. This cured most of the children. But it gave three of the children leukemia.

Gene therapy has had both happy and sad moments. Scientists are working hard to make more happy moments. For example, U.S. scientists have found a way to make new genes work in mouse muscles. They hope to cure children with muscular dystrophy in the same way. Other scientists are testing gene therapy for kidney failure and clogged blood vessels in the heart. Still others are testing gene therapy for deafness, blindness, and one dozen kinds of cancer. It'll take years before gene therapy works right every time. But when it does, it'll make a big change in medical care.

Gene Doping

The mouse on the left was genetically engineered to grow bigger and stronger than a normal mouse.

In 1998 scientists started trying gene therapy with aging mice. They wanted to slow down the muscle weakening that happens when animals get older. It worked. The mice stayed strong and fast even when they grew old and gray.

Then scientists tried the same gene therapy in young mice. The mice grew faster and bigger. They were so strong, newspapers called them "Schwarzenegger mice." (They're named after former bodybuilder Arnold Schwarzenegger, who went on to become governor of California.)

Some athletes wonder if gene therapy could help them. Could it make them run faster? Could they swim farther or lift heavier weights?

Every sport has a few athletes who cheat by using drugs to help them win. This is called doping. Most doping drugs can be found by testing an athlete's blood or urine.

People who do gene doping use human genes instead of drugs. Genes are found naturally in the human body. It may be impossible to tell if athletes have doped with genes. The World Anti-Doping Agency works to prevent the illegal use of drugs among athletes. It has already banned gene doping. But some scientists think a few athletes may already be trying it.

Some athletes cheat and use doping to help them win. Gene doping is a new way for athletes to illegally improve their performance.

Personalized Medicine

Imagine it's 2025. You take your newborn twins—a boy and a girl—home from the hospital. Their complete gene reports are stuffed into their diaper bags. (In the future, every baby's genes may be studied at birth.)

When you take your babies to their first checkup, the doctor looks at their gene reports. She sees that your son's genes put him at risk for early heart disease. Your daughter's genes show she'll get diabetes when she's older.

You and your doctor plan diet and exercise programs for your kids. These help prevent heart disease and diabetes. When your kids are older, they take drugs made just for these diseases. The twins grow up healthy. They celebrate their one-hundredth birthday together with their families!

Parents of newborn babies, like these twins, may someday be able to protect their children from genetic diseases.

Designer Babies

Parents someday may be able to design their own baby. Parents could choose everything from their baby's looks to special talents. A designer baby might be extra-good at fighting germs, so he or she would never get sick. Smart, sweet babies could become very common. Gene problems could disappear.

Scientists have already made some lab mice smarter and friendlier with gene therapy. The designer mice were healthy. The new genes didn't seem to cause them any problems.

Could scientists do the same for humans? Some people believe it would be good to help parents have the healthiest, happiest babies possible. But other people believe it would be risky and wrong to mess around with nature this way.

IT'S A FACT!

A tool called AmpliChip *(right)* studies the genes in a few drops of someone's blood. Studying someone's genes helps doctors know how that person will respond to certain drugs.

Doctors can use this tool, called an AmpliChip, to study the genes in a patient's blood.

This make-believe story isn't far from the truth. Doctors know that drugs work differently in different people. Genes help control how drugs work in each person. Doctors are studying exactly how drugs and genes work together. Knowing more about this helps doctors make good choices. They can give drugs that help people the most. They can avoid giving drugs that may hurt people.

This new kind of health care is called personalized medicine. It's already helping save lives. For example, doctors study the genes of women with ovarian cancer (cancer of the ovaries, the organs that produce eggs). This helps them figure out which powerful cancer-killing drugs will work best in their patients.

chapter 4

Sensational Stem Cells

Remember the story of Jack and the bean stalk? Imagine you have a bag of magic beans. They're even better than Jack's. They'll grow into anything you want. Say you want a new park in your neighborhood. Plant one bean, and it becomes a grassy field. Plant another one, and it grows into a row of picnic tables. Another grows into a huge tree to shade your tables. The last bean becomes a basketball court.

Stem cells are a bit like magic beans. Different body parts are made of different kinds of cells. A muscle cell is different from a skin cell. A brain cell is different from both.

Human embryonic stem cells can develop into different kinds of cells.

Stem cells are all exactly alike. They're very small, very simple cells with an amazing power. They can grow into all the body parts that make up a person. Some stem cells become a person's brain and spinal cord. Some turn into bone, muscle, and skin. Others grow into blood, finger-nails, and eyeballs.

All cells split to make copies of themselves. If you cut your finger, the healthy skin cells split and grow to replace the hurt ones. But only stem cells can create every other type of cell. Scientists have learned that stem cells can fix injuries in nearly every part of the body. Stem cells may also be able to cure many diseases. That's why the study of stem cells is so exciting.

Embryonic Stem Cells

An embryo is a baby-to-be growing inside a pregnant woman. When an embryo is five days old, it looks like a ball of cells. Stem cells are inside the ball.

Sometimes doctors help embryos form outside women's bodies. Scientists can take the stem cells out of these embryos and grow them in a dish.

These human embryonic stem cells were grown at a lab in the United Kingdom.

The Stem Cell Debate

Embryonic stem cells might heal people who are very sick or badly hurt. But not everyone thinks they should be used. Why? Because taking stem cells from embryos kills them.

Some people believe human life starts when an embryo forms. These people believe killing an embryo is the same as killing a baby.

Other people believe a ball of cells isn't the same thing as a baby. Even though it can grow into a baby, it's still only a ball of cells. These people think taking embryonic stem cells is OK if it helps people.

Adult Stem Cells

Scientists once thought only embryonic stem cells could grow into all kinds of cells. Now they know adult stem cells can sometimes do that too. Adult stem cells are those found in a person anytime after birth.

A newborn baby's umbilical cord contains blood with lots of stem cells in it. (This cord is a tube of blood vessels. It carries oxygen and food from mother to baby before birth.) At birth, a baby's cord holds about a teacup of blood. About 4 teaspoons of stem cells are in that blood.

One cord has enough stem cells to help a small child. But a bigger kid or an adult would need the stem cells from several cords. U.S. parents have about four million babies each year. Almost all their cords get

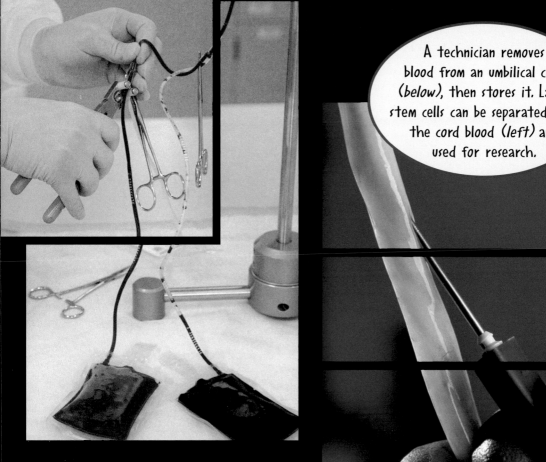

A technician removes blood from an umbilical cord (*below*), then stores it. Later, stem cells can be separated from the cord blood (*left*) and used for research.

thrown away. Most people don't know how important cord blood is. It could help a lot of people. Doctors are asking new moms to give their babies' cord blood to help others.

Bone marrow is the soft stuff inside bones. It's another good source of stem cells. Bone marrow stem cells make the different kinds of blood cells in our bodies.

Doctors have used bone marrow transplants since 1956 to help people with leukemia. The new bone marrow helps their bodies make healthy blood. Now doctors are using bone marrow stem cells to grow into nerve and muscle cells. For example, a doctor can use bone marrow stem cells to heal and strengthen a heart muscle hurt by a heart attack.

Only one in every one hundred thousand bone marrow cells is a stem cell. Scientists use a special chemical to make those few stem cells grow into enough cells to help people.

Other body organs also contain small amounts of adult stem cells. These stem cells help fix damage caused by injury and aging.

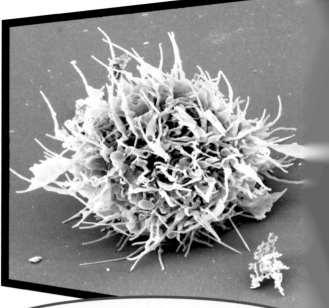

Doctors can use bone marrow stem cells like this one to treat some human diseases.

Who Can Stem Cells Help?

Stem cells can help people with many different health problems. Doctors can give people stem cells from their own bone marrow to fix damage after a heart attack. Scientists have grown new human lung cells in the lab from embryonic stem cells. They hope to help people with lung disease someday using such cells. Other scientists are testing stem cells from cord blood to see if they can cure liver disease.

One day scientists may be able to grow whole new organs for people using stem cells. Stem cell treatment looks especially hopeful for people with spine injuries and brain diseases.

Spine Injuries

Sometimes it takes a famous person to make people notice a problem. Do you remember the actor Christopher Reeve? He played Superman in four movies. In 1995 Reeve fell off a horse and hurt his spine. He was paralyzed. He could no longer move his body or feel anything below his neck.

Almost half a million people are paralyzed. Each year about eight thousand more people hurt their spines. Reeve spent the rest of his life after his fall raising money to help people with injured spines. His work sparked great interest in spine injuries.

Christopher Reeve suffered a spine injury in 1995. He is shown in 1993 (left) with his wife, Dana Reeve, and in 1996 (right). The Reeves devoted the rest of their lives to raising awareness about spine injuries.

In the years since Reeve's accident, scientists have learned a lot about using stem cells to help spine injuries. In one test, they put human stem cells into partly paralyzed mice. It worked! The stem cells formed new nerves. The mice could run again. Other scientists are giving paralyzed patients stem cells from inside their own noses. These cells may help people regrow damaged nerves.

Brain Diseases

Actor Michael J. Fox and former boxer Muhammad Ali have drawn attention to Parkinson's disease (PD). At least one million Americans have PD. Most people who get PD are over sixty years old. Sometimes younger people such as Fox get it too. PD happens when the brain can't make enough of an important chemical. PD makes people shake so

Muhammad Ali defends his World Heavyweight boxing title in 1965.

much, they can't hold a cup. They also grow stiff and can't move or talk normally. Scientists have given stem cells to animals with PD. This helped the animals move normally again.

In 2006 Muhammad Ali uses a walker to get around New York City. He suffers from Parkinson's disease.

Former president Ronald Reagan was one of four million Americans with Alzheimer's disease (AD). AD slowly and steadily kills a person's brain cells. When people get AD, they become more and more confused and forgetful. They die eight to twenty years later. Doctors wonder what would happen if they used stem cells in people with AD. Would the stem cells grow into healthy new brain cells?

IT'S A FACT!

Scientists have put human stem cells into mouse brains. The stem cells made normal mouse brain cells in the mice.

chapter 5

Teeny-Tiny Nanomedicine

What if tiny machines could race around the body killing germs? What if they could unclog blood vessels and fix broken bones? What if doctors could find cancer cells hidden deep inside the body? What if they could send drugs to kill cancer cells without hurting healthy cells?

IT'S A FACT!

A nanometer is one-billionth of a meter. A human hair is about 75,000 nanometers wide. A tiny virus is 50 nanometers wide.

When measured on the nanoscale, these human hairs seem quite large.

This 1949 computer (*above*) fills an entire room. A 2007 computer (*right*) is small enough to rest on a person's lap.

With a new science called nanotechnology, these dreams may come true. Nanotechnology is making and using tiny tools.

Scientists are always trying to make big things smaller. For example, the first computer was so big, it filled a huge room! But scientists kept working to make smaller computers. Now you can carry a laptop in your backpack.

Nanotools are so tiny that people can see them only with superstrong microscopes. Scientists build nanotools with atoms and molecules. These are the smallest bits of matter that make up all things. Some nanotools have surprising abilities. They can carry electricity or produce light.

Doctors can use nanotools to test and treat people's health problems. This is called nanomedicine.

Tiny Tests

In the 1960s' TV series *Star Trek*, Doctor McCoy ran his tricorder machine over Captain Kirk's body to figure out what was wrong. In real life, a doctor takes much longer to solve a medical puzzle. It can take days for a lab to figure out which germ is making someone sick. A doctor may ask many questions and examine a person's body. He or she may study X-rays and blood tests. The doctor still may not know what's making someone sick.

This tricorder machine from the *Star Trek* TV series was sold at an auction in 2006.

Someday nanotests will help doctors figure out people's health problems in minutes instead of hours or days. Nanotests will be faster, safer, and smarter. Doctors will no longer send tubes of blood to big labs where workers look at them under microscopes. Instead, they'll test people's bodies on the spot with nanotools. These tools will find cancer cells and germs quickly. Once a doctor knows what's wrong, treatment can start right away.

Buckyballs and quantum dots are two nanotools useful in medicine. A buckyball is a soccer ball-shaped molecule that's 1 nanometer wide. Doctors often put dyes into people to help problems show up clearly on special X-rays. But the dyes make some people sick. Buckyballs can act like little cages to protect people from the dye.

IT'S A FACT!

Doctors could use buckyballs and quantum dots in gene therapy to send genes into human cells.

Quantum dots are 5-nanometer metal crystals. They can make light. Doctors can coat quantum dots with cancer antibodies. Then they put the dots into people who have cancer. The quantum dots find the cancer cells and make them glow under special lights. The glow helps doctors see exactly where the cancer cells are.

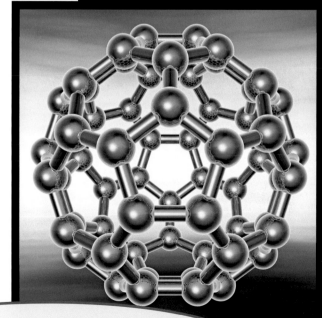

Buckyballs, as seen in this illustration, may someday be very important in gene therapy and research.

Doctors are already using nanomedicine to treat cancer patients. Many people with cancer get chemotherapy (strong cancer-fighting drugs given to the whole body). These drugs are good at killing cancer cells. But the drugs also kill healthy cells. That makes people very sick. Nanomedicine lets doctors send the drugs to cancer cells only. Imagine tiny hollow balls filled with cancer drugs. These balls find and enter a tumor (a place where many cancer cells grow together). The balls release the drugs inside the tumor. That way, they kill only the cancer cells.

An idea in development is to attach shells made of gold atoms to tiny glass beads. Doctors could add cancer antibodies to the shells and put them into the body. Within hours the shells gather at a tumor. Doctors aim a special beam of light at the tumor. The light heats up the shells and kills the tumor. This method has cured cancer in lab mice. Doctors could also use it to search for stray cancer cells left over after other kinds of treatment.

Nanomedicine could protect people as well as cure them. When people get sick or grow older, their cells release chemicals called free radicals. Free radicals damage our cells. Vitamins C and E "eat up" small amounts of free radicals. But scientists have found that buckyballs are much better at this than vitamins. When used in people with heart problems and diabetes, buckyballs might soak up free radicals like thirsty sponges. This may also help prevent some kinds of cancer.

The Promise of Cutting-Edge Medicine

Weird drugs, new transplants, gene therapy, stem cells, and nanomedicine are not just dreams. Doctors are already using these exciting medical tools. Surgeons have transplanted entire arms. Gene therapy has cured children with terrible diseases. Stem cells have strengthened heart muscles weakened by heart attacks. Nanomedicine is helping doctors find and treat cancer better than ever.

Six-month-old Chong Lih Ying raises her transplanted arm five months after surgery.

What will health care be like when you grow up? Gene problems might be cured at birth. Doctors may not need to cut into bodies to fix injured organs. New body parts might be grown from people's own cells. Diseases that spread from person to person, such as flu and AIDS, could be prevented or easily cured. Other diseases, such as cancer, diabetes, and heart disease, might disappear.

An American baby born in 1900 lived about forty-seven years. Babies born in 1950 could expect to live sixty-eight years. Those born in 2002 can expect to live seventy-seven years. Perhaps babies born in 2025 will live to be 125 years old. Cutting-edge medicine will help people live longer and healthier lives.

Glossary

antibiotic: a drug that fights bacteria

antibody: protein that attacks invaders in the body, such as germs

atom: the smallest building block of matter

buckyball: soccer ball–shaped molecule that's 1 nanometer wide

chemotherapy: strong cancer-fighting drugs given to the whole body

embryo: name for a baby-to-be growing inside a pregnant woman

gene: tiny chemical bundles inside all cells that tell the cells exactly how to do everything they need to live

gene therapy: treatment of disease by replacing sick genes with healthy ones

molecule: smallest unit of any material, made of one or more atoms

nanomedicine: use of nanotools (tiny tools) in health care

nanotechnology: making and using tiny tools

quantum dot: 5-nanometer metal crystal that can make light

reject: attack a transplanted part

stem cell: simple cell that can grow into any kind of cell

vaccine: drug that helps the body fight disease-causing germs by making antibodies against them

Selected Bibliography

Booker, Richard, and Earl Boysen. *Nanotechnology for Dummies.* Indianapolis: Wiley Publishing, 2005.

Cheater, Mark. "Chasing the Magic Dragon." *National Wildlife Federation.* N.d. http://www.nwf.org/nationalwildlife/article.cfm?articleId=810&issueId=63 (February 18, 2007).

Hitti, Miranda. "Stem Cells: 11 Questions and Answers." *WebMD.* October 27, 2006. http://www.webmd.com/content/article/129/117295.htm (February 18, 2007).

National Cancer Institute. "Understanding Nanodevices." *National Cancer Institute.* N.d. http://www.cancer.gov/cancertopics/understandingcancer/nanodevices (February 18, 2007).

National Human Genome Research Institute. "Genetics: The Future of Medicine." *The Human Genome Project: Exploring Our Molecular Selves.* N.d. http://www.genome.gov/Pages/EducationKit/brochure.html (February 18, 2007).

National Institutes of Health. "Stem Cell Basics." *Stem Cell Information.* December 20, 2006. http://stemcells.nih.gov/info/basics (February 18, 2007).

National Parkinson Foundation. "About Parkinson Disease." *National Parkinson Foundation.* N.d. http://www.parkinson.org/site/pp.asp?c=9dJFJLPwB&b=71125 (February 18, 2007).

National Spinal Cord Injury Association. "More about Spinal Cord Injury." *The National Spinal Cord Injury Association.* N.d. http://www.spinalcord.org/html/factsheets/spinstat.php (February 18, 2007).

Rados, Carol. "Beyond Bloodletting: FDA Gives Leeches a Medical Makeover." *U.S. Food and Drug Administration.* 2004. http://www.fda.gov/fdac/features/2004/504_leech.html (February 18, 2007).

Shnayerson, Michael, and Mark Plotkin. *The Killers Within: The Deadly Rise of Drug-Resistant Bacteria.* Boston: Little, Brown and Company, 2002.

Weintraub, Arlene. "Stem Cells to Go." *BusinessWeek Online.* June 27, 2005. http://www.businessweek.com/magazine/content/05_26/b3939099_mz018.htm (February 18, 2007).

Alliance for the Prudent Use of Antibiotics. http://www.tufts.edu/med/apua. This website explains how antibiotics work and how to keep these important drugs working as long as possible.

Christopher Reeve Foundation. http://www.christopherreeve.org. This organization is dedicated to curing spinal cord injuries by funding research and improving the quality of life for people with paralysis. Its website offers paralysis research news as well as help and information on living with paralysis.

Fridell, Ron. *Genetic Engineering.* Minneapolis: Lerner Publications Company, 2006. Fridell's book describes how genetic engineering affects our lives and how it may help us in the future.

Goldsmith, Connie. *Superbugs Strike Back: When Antibiotics Fail.* Minneapolis: Twenty-First Century Books, 2007. This book explains how some dangerous bacteria resist antibiotic drugs and how doctors are looking for new antibiotics to help us fight these germs.

Johnson, Rebecca. *Nanotechnology.* Minneapolis: Lerner Publications Company, 2006. This book explains how scientists build tiny tools from atoms and molecules, and it describes some of the amazing jobs these tools can do.

The Michael J. Fox Foundation for Parkinson's Research. http://www.michaeljfox.org. This organization is devoted to finding a cure for Parkinson's disease by encouraging and funding research. Its website provides lots of information about Parkinson's disease and news on Parkinson's research.

NanoKids. http://cohesion.rice.edu/naturalsciences/nanokids. This interactive website helps kids understand the science of nanotechnology.

National Nanotechnology Initiative. http://www.nano.gov. This U.S. government organization encourages nanotechnology by funding research. Its website discusses how nanotools are built and used.

Stem Cell Information. http://stemcells.nih.gov. This U.S. National Institutes of Health website explains in detail stem cells and stem cell research.

Stem Cell Research Foundation. http://www.stemcellresearchfoundation.org. This website offers the latest news in stem cell research and discusses how stem cells may improve our health in the future.

Index

Photo Acknowledgments

The images in this book are used with the permission of: PhotoDisc Royalty Free by Getty Images, pp. 1, 10 (top), all page backgrounds; © Alexis Rosenfeld/Photo Researchers, Inc., p. 5; © Hulton Archive/Getty Images, p. 6 (both); © Mediscan/Visuals Unlimited, p. 7 (both); © Torsten Blackwood/AFP/Getty Images, p. 8; © Jim Merli/Visuals Unlimited, p. 9; St. Bartholomew's Hospital/Photo Researchers, Inc., p. 10 (bottom left); © Volker Steger/Photo Researchers, Inc., p. 10 (bottom right); © BananaStock Ltd., p. 12; © Vince Bucci/AFP/Getty Images, p. 14; © Dominique Duval/Photo Researchers, Inc., p. 17; © Scientifica/Visuals Unlimited, p. 18; © CHU Amiens via Getty Images, p. 19; AP Photo/Jamie Martin, p. 21; AP Photo/Associazione Luca Coscioni, p. 22; AP Photo/Muscular Dystrophy Association, Jay LaPrete, p. 23; AP Photo, pp. 24, 39 (top); AP Photo/Keith Weller, p. 25; © Carl Purcell/Photo Researchers, Inc., p. 26; © Margaret Miller/Photo Researchers, Inc., p. 27; © 1996-2007 F. Hoffman-La Roche Ltd. AmpliChip is a trademark of Roche Molecular Systems, Inc., p. 28; © James Cavallini/Photo Researchers, Inc., p. 30 (both); © Professor Miodrag Stojkovic/Photo Researchers, Inc., p. 31 (both); © William Perlman/Star Ledger/CORBIS, p. 33 (left); © James King-Holmes/Photo Researchers, Inc., p. 33 (right); © Gary D. Gaugler/Photo Researchers, Inc., p. 34; © DMI/Time & Life Pictures/Getty Images, p. 35 (left); © Tim Clary/AFP/Getty Images, p. 35 (right); © Central Press/Hulton Archive/Getty Images, p. 36 (all); © Arnaldo Magnani/Getty Images, p. 37 (all); © George Musil/Visuals Unlimited, p. 38; © Karlene Schwartz, p. 39 (bottom right); © Bruno Vincent/Getty Images, p. 40; © Matthias Kulka/zefa/CORBIS, p. 41; © Reuters/CORBIS, p. 43.

Front Cover: © Dennis Kunkel Microscopy, Inc. (left); © Bruce Dale/National Geographic/Getty Images (top right); Comstock Images (bottom right); PhotoDisc Royalty Free by Getty Images (background).

About the Author

Connie Goldsmith is a registered nurse with a bachelor of science degree in nursing and a master of public administration degree in health care. She is the author of *Influenza; Invisible Invaders: Dangerous Infectious Diseases;* and *Superbugs Strike Back: When Antibiotics Fail*. She has also published more than two hundred magazine articles, mostly on health topics for adults and children. She lives near Sacramento, California.

OCT 2010

Published in the United States by Little, Brown and Company,
34 Beacon Street, Boston, Massachusetts, 02106.
Originally published in Great Britain by Walker Books Ltd., London.

First American Edition

Library of Congress Catalog Card Number: 86-80447

Printed in Italy

ISBN 0-316-54005-6

SHAPES

ROSALINDA KIGHTLEY

LITTLE, BROWN AND COMPANY
BOSTON/TORONTO

circle

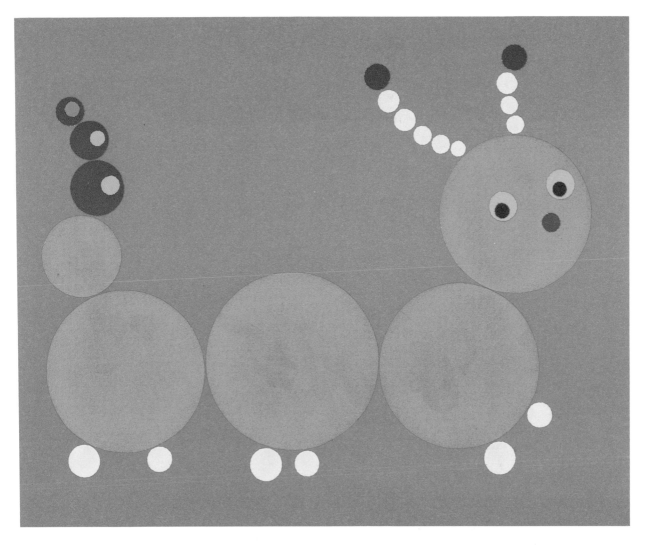

How many circles can you find?

square

How many squares can you find?

rectangle

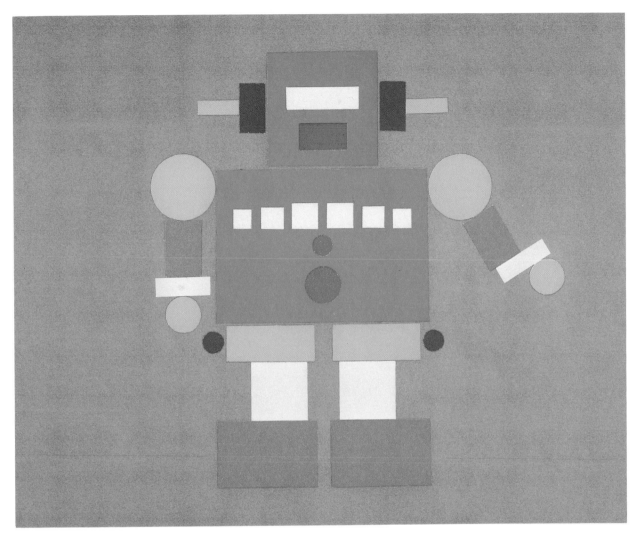

How many rectangles can you find?

triangle

How many triangles can you find?

diamond

How many diamonds can you find?

semicircle

How many semicircles can you find?

straight line

How many straight lines can you find?

right angle

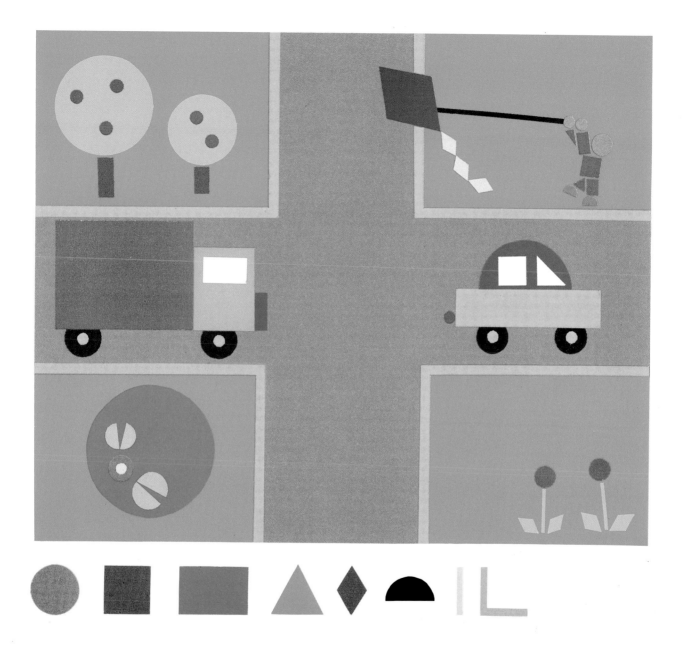

How many right angles can you find?

zigzag

How many zizags can you find?

wavy line

How many wavy lines can you find?

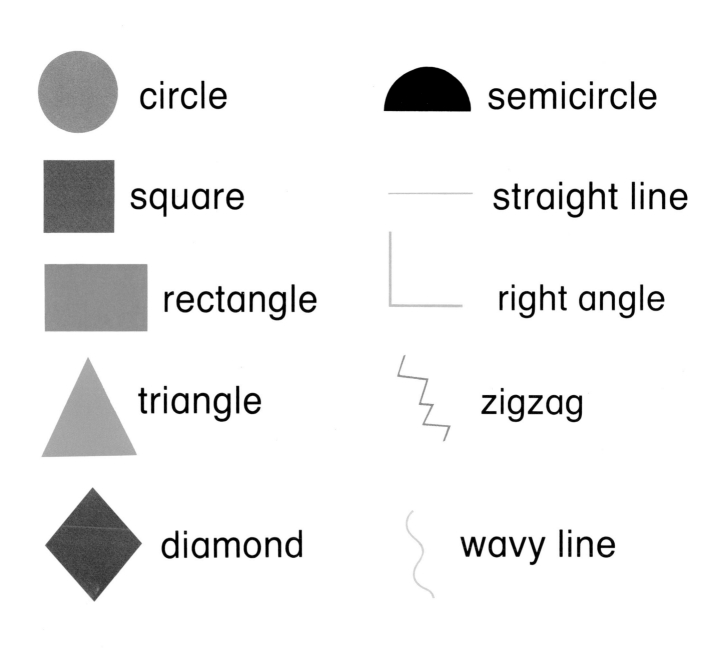

circle

semicircle

square

straight line

rectangle

right angle

triangle

zigzag

diamond

wavy line

How many shapes can you find?

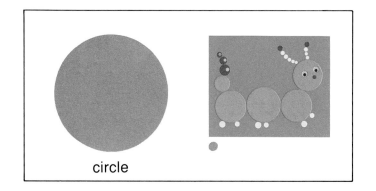

circle

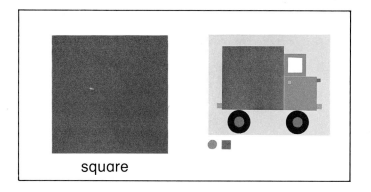

square

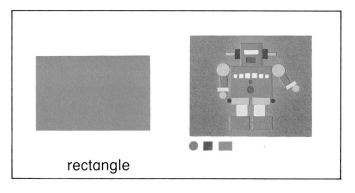

rectangle

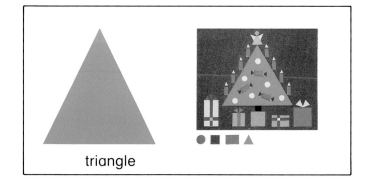

triangle

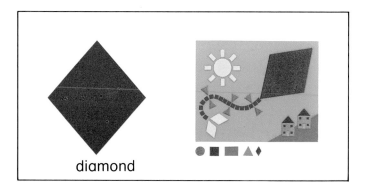

diamond

semicircle

straight line

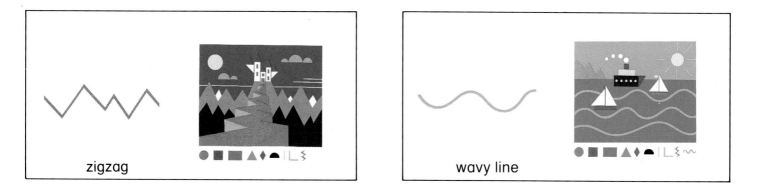

right angle

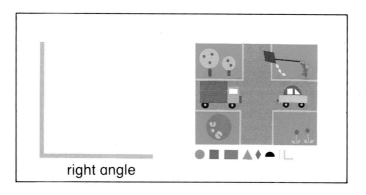

zigzag

wavy line